Usborne

Animal Picture Atlas

Illustrated by Linda Edwards
Written by Hazel Maskell

Designed by Amanda Gulliver
and Nicola Butler

Edited by Gillian Doherty
Consultants: Dr. Margaret Rostron and Dr. John Rostron
Cartographer: Craig Asquith

Contents

About this book

This book is all about animals and where they live.

The first part is full of maps showing different areas of the world and some of the animals that live there.

The second part gives more information about particular kinds of animals. There are also animals to spot on the maps, and at the back you'll find an animal quiz to try.

The world

Animals live all around the world, on the land, in the sky and in the oceans. This map shows just a few of the most amazing ones.

Arctic Circle

ARCTIC OCEAN

NORTH AMERICA

Blue whales are the biggest animals.

Peregrine falcons are the fastest birds.

Salmon live in the oceans, but swim huge distances to lay their eggs in rivers and lakes.

Bee hummingbirds are the tiniest birds.

Giant squids have the biggest eyes of any animal.

African elephants are the biggest land animals.

Goliath beetles are the biggest insects.

Equator

The Equator is a line added to maps to show where the middle of the Earth is.

Giant tortoises can live for over 150 years.

SOUTH AMERICA

Swordfish use their long, sharp spikes to slash their prey.

PACIFIC OCEAN

Black swallowers have stretchy stomachs, so they can eat animals bigger than themselves.

NORTH

WEST   EAST

SOUTH

The compasses on the maps show which way north, south, east and west are.

ATLANTIC OCEAN

Albatrosses are the birds with the biggest wingspans.

Antarctic Circle

4

The shading on the maps shows what the land is like in different parts of the world and where there are rivers, lakes, seas and oceans.

ice and snow   deserts   grasslands   forests   mountains   rivers and lakes   seas and oceans

Male narwhals' tusks are much longer than an adult human is tall.

Arctic Circle

EUROPE

Water shrews have venom in their spit.

Pandas are very rare, with only a few thousand left in the wild.

ASIA

PACIFIC OCEAN

AFRICA

Whale sharks are the biggest fish.

Cheetahs are the fastest runners.

Equator

Giraffes are the tallest animals.

Reticulated pythons can be longer than five humans lying head to toe.

Platypuses and spiny anteaters are the only animals with hair that lay eggs.

INDIAN OCEAN

Box jellyfish are the animals with the most deadly venom.

AUSTRALASIA AND OCEANIA

Ostriches are the biggest birds.

Kiwis have nostrils on the end of their beaks.

Sperm whales can hold their breath for over an hour and a half.

The largest animals that live on Antarctica all year round are tiny insects called midges.

Antarctic Circle

5

ANTARCTICA

North America

6

ARCTIC OCEAN

PACIFIC OCEAN

GREENLAND

CANADA

ALASKA (USA)

UNITED STATES OF AMERICA

Arctic Circle

NUUK (GODTHAB)

MONTREAL

ANCHORAGE

VANCOUVER

SEATTLE

SAN FRANCISCO

Gulf of Alaska

Hudson Bay

The Great Lakes

Rocky Mountains

Missouri River

Brent goose

stoat

Canada goose

minke whale

lobster

snapping turtle

American black bear

cod

ptarmigan

snowy owl

cardinal

blue jay

Arctic terns

beluga whale

great blue heron

wolf

skunk

beaver

Arctic hare

musk ox

moose

mink

buffalo

sage grouse

Arctic char

brown bear

mountain goat

pronghorn

snow goose

muskrat

pika

bald eagle

burrowing owl

polar bear

Caribou

bighorn sheep

raccoon

walrus

Pacific salmon

orca

sea otter

ATLANTIC
OCEAN

tiger
salamander

herrings

WASHINGTON DC
NEW YORK

CHICAGO

red-tailed
hawk

porcupine

Arizona desert
scorpion

LOS ANGELES

Colorado River

rattlesnake

prairie dog

coyote

roadrunner

Rio Grande River

gila monster

MEXICO

free-tailed
bat

monarch
butterfly

MEXICO CITY

elephant
seal

common
dolphins

great white
shark

cottontail
rabbit

bobcat

long-horned
cattle

black widow
spider

alligator

Gulf of
Mexico

Mississippi River

turkey
vulture

red snappers

ringtail

marlin

stingrays

Leeward
Islands

Puerto Rico

THE
BAHAMAS

CUBA

HAVANA

spoonbill

hutia

JAMAICA

HAITI

DOMINICAN
REPUBLIC

Caribbean
monk seal

Caribbean Sea

angel fish

leaf-
cutter
ant

BELIZE
BELMOPAN

GUATEMALA

GUATEMALA CITY

HONDURAS
TEGUCIGALPA

NICARAGUA

EL SALVADOR
SAN SALVADOR

MANAGUA

COSTA
RICA

SAN JOSE

PANAMA
PANAMA CITY

howler
monkey

sea
turtle

giant
tortoise

Galapagos Islands
(South America)

PACIFIC
OCEAN

Windward
Islands

TRINIDAD
AND
TOBAGO

NORTH
EAST
WEST
SOUTH

■ Capital cities
● Other big cities

The world

NORTH
AMERICA

This map shows where North America is.

South America

NORTH
EAST
WEST
SOUTH

Equator

white shark

thresher shark

Caribbean Sea

rufous-tailed hummingbird

shrimps

dorado

scarlet ibis

iguana

CARACAS

VENEZUELA

Orinoco River

puma

COLOMBIA

BOGOTA

saki monkey

peccary

tapir

QUITO

ECUADOR

fruit bat

condor

PERU

Andes Mountains

LIMA

dragonfish

CAYENNE

FRENCH GUIANA

SURINAM

PARAMARIBO

GEORGETOWN

GUYANA

caiman

sloth

cane toad

red brocket

poison dart frog

pygmy marmoset

Amazon River

piranha

Amazon Rainforest

blue morpho butterfly

heliconid butterfly

spider monkey

llama

guinea pig

coati

ocelot

harpy eagle

spectacled owl

capuchin monkey

pampas deer

Brazilian wandering spider

rainbow boa

Sao Francisco River

Tocantins River

BRASILIA

BRAZIL

armadillo

capybara

toucan

anaconda

jaguar

agouti

scarlet macaw

Tapajos River

tarantula

river dolphin

Madeira River

spectacled bear

BOLIVIA

mountain cat

LA PAZ

SUCRE

jabiru

ATLANTIC OCEAN

deep-sea anglerfish

mackerel

sardines

RÍO DE JANEIRO

orange roughy

The world

SOUTH AMERICA

This map shows where South America is.

South Georgia

SAO PAULO

golden lion tamarin

tarpon

sardines

maned wolf

PARAGUAY

ASUNCION

URUGUAY

MONTEVIDEO

king crab

albatrosses

Falkland Islands

giant anteater

Paraná River

BUENOS AIRES

chinchilla

ARGENTINA

rhea

hornero

mara

guanaco

Magellan penguin

sea lions

Cape Horn

Atacama Desert

degu

CHILE

SANTIAGO

huemel

Andes Mountains

fur seal

rockhopper penguin

flamingos

opah

southern right whale

PACIFIC OCEAN

mackerel

■ Capital cities
● Other big cities

9

Australasia and Oceania

PACIFIC OCEAN

NORTH
WEST   EAST
SOUTH

Northern Mariana Islands

Moorish idol

PALAU

sea cucumber

FEDERATED STATES OF MICRONESIA

Equator

dugong

spiny bandicoot

crowned pigeon

tree kangaroo

cuscus

blue bird of paradise

PAPUA NEW GUINEA

■ PORT MORESBY

clownfish

pineapple fish

box jellyfish

Children's python

coral

harlequin fish

spiny anteater

termites

possum

frilled lizard

Great Barrier Reef

butterfly fish

bilby

koalas

humpback grouper

thorny devil

AUSTRALIA

kangaroos

blue-ringed octopus

cockatiel

wallaby

Great Victoria Desert

redback spider

Darling River

platypus

bottlenose dolphin

dingo

emu

wombat

parakeet

● SYDNEY

bowerbirds

CANBERRA

blue-tongued skink

snake-necked turtle

● PERTH

galah

MELBOURNE

sea dragon

crayfish

black swan

Tasmania

great white shark

Tasmanian devil

■ Capital cities
● Other big cities

10

spinner
dolphins

apapane

Hawaiian Islands

reef
triggerfish

fairy terns

PACIFIC
OCEAN

MARSHALL
ISLANDS

black
swallower

blue shark

green
turtles

NAURU

moray eel

flying
fish

Equator

KIRIBATI

SOLOMON
ISLANDS

hatchetfish

parrotfish

manta
rays

TUVALU

Tokelau

brown
booby

VANUATU

golden
dove

Wallis and
Futuna

SAMOA

rainbow
lorikeet

American
Samoa

tuna

giant grouper

FIJI

TONGA

Niue

sea
horses

tropic
bird

French Polynesia

Caledonia

swordfish

Cook Islands

Tahiti

bluestripe
snappers

The world

barracudas

giant squid

kiwi

NEW
ZEALAND

weta

■ WELLINGTON

AUSTRALASIA
AND OCEANIA

This map shows where Australasia
and Oceania are.

sheep

hoki

beaked whale

Asia

herring

water
shrew

kittiwake

lynx

nutcracker

MOSCOW ■

Ural Mountains

noctule bat

flying
squirrel

redback
vole

golden
eagle

weasel

Volga River

honey bee

ASTANA ■

dwarf
hamster

bactrian
camel

sand
lizard

Caspian seal

*Aral
Sea*

KAZAKHSTAN

jerboa

MONGOLIA

Dalmatian
pelican

*Black
Sea*

*Caspian
Sea*

great
bustard

BISHKEK

ISTANBUL ●

GEORGIA

UZBEKISTAN

KYRGYZSTAN

goitered
gazelle

*Gobi
Desert*

ANKARA ■

ARMENIA

TASHKENT ■

trap-door
spider

TURKEY

AZERBAIJAN

TURKMENISTAN

TAJIKISTAN

snow
leopard

Cyprus

SYRIA

TEHRAN ●

ASHGABAT ■

LEBANON

Bezoar's
goat

IRAN

jackal

red panda

yak

ISRAEL

DAMASCUS ■

desert
hedgehog

KABUL ■

JERUSALEM ■

BAGHDAD ●

AFGHANISTAN

JORDAN

IRAQ

ISLAMABAD ■

The Himalayas

KUWAIT

hyena

long-legged
buzzard

PAKISTAN

Indus River

sloth bears

NEW DELHI ■

NEPAL

*Mount
Everest*

Ganges River

KATHMANDU ■

BHUTAN

RIYADH ■

QATAR

blackbuck

BANGLADESH

stonefish

UNITED ARAB
EMIRATES

MUSCAT ■

INDIA

DHAKA ■

dhole

MECCA ●

SAUDI
ARABIA

OMAN

giant
squirrel

BURMA

Red Sea

Arabian
horse

finless
porpoise

BOMBAY ●

Bengal tiger

Russell's
viper

SANA ■

Arabian
camel

RANGOON ●

YEMEN

*Arabian
Sea*

Asian
elephant

NORTH

zebu

peacock

Andaman
Islands

WEST

Socotra

EAST

sun
bear

SOUTH

hawksbill
turtles

SRI LANKA

COLOMBO ■

KUALA LUM

SRI JAYEWARDENEPURA KOTTE

Maldives

Equator

elegant
unicornfish

mouse
deer

striped dolphin

coral

■ Capital cities

● Other big cities

soldier
fish

tiger shark

reticulated
python

12

*INDIAN
OCEAN*

beluga whale

narwhal

ringed seal

lemming

walrus

snow goose

willow grouse

little auk

Bering Sea

bearded seal

bowhead whales

RUSSIA

black woodpecker

Sea of Okhotsk

spiny dogfish

sockeye salmon

sea lion

Siberian toad

raccoon dog

Asiatic black bear

sika deer

sperm whale

pollock

LAN BATOR

crested ibis

black vulture

VLADIVOSTOK

spider crab

PACIFIC OCEAN

Yellow River

BEIJING

NORTH KOREA

PYONGYANG

JAPAN

puffer fish

white-sided dolphin

praying mantis

SEOUL

SOUTH KOREA

TOKYO

CHINA

Yangtze River

giant panda

oakleaf butterfly

rhesus macaque

TAIPEI

mandarin duck

Japanese crane

The world

IETNAM

HANOI

HONG KONG

TAIWAN

octopus

ASIA

LAOS

ENTIANE

South China Sea

clown triggerfish

Philippine Sea

THAILAND

MANILA

CAMBODIA

HNOM PENH

THE PHILIPPINES

sea krait

tarsier

manta ray

This map shows where Asia is.

LAYSIA

BRUNEI

JGAPORE

Borneo

giant clam

Equator

matra

orangutans

Celebes

New Guinea

INDONESIA

JAKARTA

Java

EAST TIMOR

Komodo dragon

Arafura Sea

13

Africa

ATLANTIC OCEAN

Mediterranean Sea

Moroccan orange-tip

Madeira

Canary Islands

■ ALGIERS

■ TUNIS
TUNISIA

RABAT ■

■ TRIPOLI

MOROCCO

Atlas Mountains

Barbary sheep

fennec fox

sandgrouse

LAAYOUNE ■

WESTERN SAHARA

ground squirrel

ALGERIA

locust

horned viper

Sahara Desert

bottlenose dolphin

MAURITANIA

MALI

dromedary

NIGER

fat-tailed scorpion

gerbil

tripod fish

NOUAKCHOTT ■

Niger River

Cape Verde Islands

hippopotamus

bee-eater

SENEGAL

DAKAR ■

NIAMEY ■

THE GAMBIA

baboons

GUINEA-BISSAU

BAMAKO ■

BURKINA FASO

zor

GUINEA

NDJAMENA

NIGERIA

honeyguide

BENIN

honey badger

CONAKRY ■

TOGO

FREETOWN ■

bongo

YAMOUSSOUKRO

ABUJA ■

SIERRA LEONE

GHANA

● LAGOS

MONROVIA ■

IVORY COAST

ACCRA ■

mandrill

BANGU

snipe eel

LIBERIA

YAOUNDE ●

CAMEROON

deep-sea eel

EQUATORIAL GUINEA

Equator

LIBREVILLE ■

REPUBLIC OF THE CONGO

GABON

chimpanzee

BRAZZAVILLE ●

KINSHA

ATLANTIC OCEAN

flying fish

ANGOLA

LUANDA ■

oryx

meerkats

anchovies

millipede

NAMIBI

WINDHOEK ■

The world

AFRICA

This map shows where Africa is.

■ Capital cities
● Other big cities

manx shearwater

ostri

CAPE TOW

Risso's dolphin

dorcas
gazelle

LIBYA

CAIRO

Nile River

Egyptian
cobra

quail

EGYPT

Red Sea

Nubian Desert

HAD

crocodile

KHARTOUM

ERITREA

ASMARA

SUDAN

ETHIOPIA

DJIBOUTI

SOMALIA

hoopoe

oarfish

leopard tortoise

scarab
beetle

ADDIS
ABABA

CENTRAL
AFRICAN
REPUBLIC

rhinoceros

giraffe

wild
donkey

leopard

INDIAN
OCEAN

DEMOCRATIC
REPUBLIC OF
THE CONGO

Congo River

UGANDA

zebra

MOGADISHU

KAMPALA

Lake
Victoria

KENYA

NAIROBI

secretary
bird

Equator

RWANDA

lion

Zanzibar
butterfly fish

frigate
bird

BURUNDI

gorilla

TANZANIA

DODOMA

DAR ES SALAAM

hammerhead shark

African
elephant

zebra shark

SEYCHELLES

cheetah

oriental
sweetlips fish

ZAMBIA

MALAWI

LUSAKA

Zambezi River

LILONGWE

chameleon

hbaby

ZIMBABWE

HARARE

aardvark

aye-aye

impala

MOZAMBIQUE

ANTANANARIVO

MAURITIUS

NORTH

BOTSWANA
Kalahari
Desert

sunbird

MADAGASCAR

cow fish

ABORONE

stick
insect

PRETORIA

MAPUTO

WEST

EAST

JOHANNESBURG

SWAZILAND

ring-tailed
lemur

BLOEMFONTEIN

LESOTHO

jellyfish

SOUTH

SOUTH AFRICA

15

rock hyraxes

Europe

ARCTIC
OCEAN

Arctic Circle

REYKJAVIK ■ ICELAND

gyrfalcon

blue whale

cod

Faroe
Islands

sea urchin

white-tailed
eagle

fjord
pony

NORWAY

OSLO

humpback
whale

halibut

Shetland
Islands

common
toad

ATLANTIC
OCEAN

Atlantic
salmon

NORTH

WEST   EAST

SOUTH

otter

UNITED
KINGDOM

gannets

bad

DENMARK

COPENHAG

European
robin

DUBLIN ■

IRELAND

water vole

North
Sea

garden
spider

European
rabbit

guillemots

hedgehog

stag
beetle

NETHERLANDS

AMSTERDAM ■
LONDON ■   THE HAGUE

BERLIN

sei whale

dragonfly

Eurasian jay

BRUSSELS

BELGIUM

black-bellied
hamster

cuttlefish

harvest
mouse

PARIS ■

LUXEMBOURG

GERMANY

pipistrelle
bat

mussels

barn
owl

oysters

Bay of
Biscay

FRANCE

BERN ■

AUSTRI

SWITZERLAND

■ Capital cities
● Other big cities

polecat

pheasant

asp viper

The
Alps

SLOVENIA

sponge

PORTUGAL

Montpellier
snake

ANDORRA

Alpine marmot

Corsica

LISBON ■

MADRID ■

SPAIN

wild cat

sole

Sardinia

green
woodpecker

ROME
■

ITAL

tree frog

red kite

eyed
lizard

red mullet

mouflon

Madeira

basking shark

Mediterranean Sea

Sicily

16

Canary
Islands

Mooris
gecko

MALTA

greater argentine

flounder

puffins

reindeer

wolverine

SWEDEN

crossbill

brown rat

capercaillie

Siberian chipmunk

Ural Mountains

sparrow hawk

whooper swan

sable

Ural owl

goldeneye

RUSSIA

moose

red squirrel

FINLAND

Baltic Sea

cuckoo

hawkmoth

greylag goose

woodlouse spider

brown hare

HELSINKI ■

■ STOCKHOLM

■ TALLINN

ESTONIA

mallards

sprats

RIGA

LATVIA

red fox

MOSCOW

LITHUANIA

mole

VILNIUS ■

shore crab

MINSK ■

moor frog

Volga River

POLAND

BELARUS

wild boar

grass snake

black stork

■ WARSAW

European bison

fallow deer

KIEV ■

Dnieper River

molerat

Don River

nightingale

chamois

UKRAINE

corncrake

ZECH PUBLIC

NNA

SLOVAKIA

Carpathian Mountains

crested newt

BRATISLAVA

MOLDOVA

BUDAPEST

ROMANIA

CHISINAU

HUNGARY

apollo butterfly

European kingfisher

ROATIA

BUCHAREST

BOSNIA & ERZEGOVINA

SERBIA

BELGRADE ■

Danube River

■

sturgeon

Black Sea

ARAJEVO

MONTENEGRO

SOFIA ■

PODGORICA

BULGARIA

souslik

corpionfish

MACEDONIA

TURKEY

■ ISTANBUL

TIRANA ■

ALBANIA

GREECE

wolf spider

Aesculapian snake

lammergeier

ATHENS ■

Mediterranean monk seal

Crete

The world

EUROPE

This map shows where Europe is.

17

The Arctic

Bering Sea

sea eagle

Sea of Okhotsk

Northern fur seal

Gulf of Alaska

spectacled eider

snow sheep

Arctic ground squirrel

ALASKA

bearded seal

Chukchi Sea

CANADA

malamute

moose

Wrangel Island

walrus

Siberian tiger

wolf

purple heron

Arctic loon

Beaufort Sea

New Siberia Islands

Laptev Sea

RUSSIA

ARCTIC OCEAN

snowy owl

Arctic terns

narwhal

lynx

Canada goose

Arctic fox

NORTH POLE

Severnaya Zemlya

Arctic hare

lemming

stoat

Arctic Circle

Ellesmere Island

ringed seal

Kara Sea

Baffin Island

Franz Josef Land

polar bear

hooded seal

Novaya Zemlya

Arctic chars

caribou

harp seal

Svalbard reindeer

Barents Sea

GREENLAND

■ NUUK (GODTHAB)

minke whale

musk ox

The world

ARCTIC

ptarmigan

puffins

REYKJAVIK ■ ICELAND

ANTARCTICA

The Arctic and Antarctica are on opposite sides of the world.

ATLANTIC OCEAN

fulmar

18

skate

Antarctica

SOUTHERN OCEAN

AFRICA is this way.

blue whale

sea bass

South Georgia

king penguin

ATLANTIC OCEAN

macaroni penguin

blue-eyed shag

krill

INDIAN OCEAN

snail fish

dove prions

SOUTH AMERICA is this way.

Weddell Sea

giant petrels

crabeater seal

Adélie penguin

colossal squid

Antarctic Peninsula

Ronne Ice Shelf

fur seal

ANTARCTICA

Weddell seal

anemone

midges

SOUTH POLE

elephant seal

brittle star

Transantarctic Mountains

Ross Ice Shelf

Ross Sea

Antarctic Circle

Ross seal

emperor penguins

toothfish

icefish

soft coral

snow petrel

PACIFIC OCEAN

AUSTRALIA is this way.

salmon shark

SOUTHERN OCEAN

19

chinstrap penguin

orca

rockhopper penguin

Arctic terns

Monkeys and apes

Monkeys and apes mainly live in forests in Asia, Africa and South America. They have hands with long fingers that can grasp and carry things. Most monkeys also have tails, but apes don't.

Gentle giants

Apes are bigger than monkeys, and gorillas are the biggest apes of all. They can look scary, but really they are peaceful plant-eaters. Even the huge males only fight occasionally, usually to protect their families.

A gorilla family is made up of an adult male called a silverback, several females and their babies.

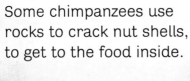

Some chimpanzees use rocks to crack nut shells, to get to the food inside.

Intelligent chimpanzees

Chimpanzees are very clever apes. They know how to use objects such as sticks and leaves to collect food and water. They also tell each other things by making faces and noises.

Can you find these monkeys and apes on the maps?

golden lion tamarin
Look in
South America

saki monkey
Look in
South America

pygmy marmoset
Look in
South America

orangutans
Look in
Asia

Expert climbers

As monkeys and apes move along branches, they clutch them with their long fingers and toes. Some also use their arms, legs or tails to help them to swing from tree to tree.

A spider monkey can hang from its long, strong tail as it collects fruit.

A group leader growls and bares its teeth to show it's in charge.

Group life

Most monkeys and apes live in groups. Some groups have over a hundred members, while others are just small families. There is usually a strict order of importance within each group.

Friendly cleaners

Monkeys and apes spend hours grooming one another's fur. This keeps them clean and they also enjoy it, so it's a good way of bonding with other group members.

Monkeys pick dirt and mites from each other's coats.

capuchin monkey
Look in
South America

mandrill
Look in
Africa

baboons
Look in
Africa

rhesus macaque
Look in
Asia

Big cats

With their sharp teeth and claws, cats are superb hunters. Like all hunters, they catch other animals, called prey, to eat. The biggest cats live in Africa, Asia and South America.

Team hunting

Lions are the only cats that live in groups. The females hunt together to catch the group's food, and the males protect the group from danger.

Lions hunt at night, and spend their days resting and dozing.

Up in the trees, a leopard has a good view and can watch out for prey.

Hiding food

Leopards spend most of their time in treetops. They come down to hunt, but drag their food back up into the branches to hide it from other animals that might steal it.

Can you find these cats on the maps?

lion
Look in
Africa

cheetah
Look in
Africa

ocelot
Look in
South America

puma
Look in
South America

A tiger's stripes blend in with the tall grasses, making it hard to see.

Stealthy hunters

Tigers are silent, watchful hunters. They hide among bushes or tall grasses and stalk their prey, gradually creeping closer until they are near enough to pounce.

Fast runners

Cheetahs live in flat grasslands, and they run incredibly quickly to catch their prey. But they get so hot that they can only run for short distances before stopping.

As a cheetah runs, it stretches out its long legs to take huge strides.

leopard
Look in
Africa

Bengal tiger
Look in
Asia

jaguar
Look in
South America

snow leopard
Look in
Asia

Bears

Bears live in North America, South
America, Asia and Europe. They are
powerful animals, and some can kill with
one swipe of their huge paws. They can
also run quickly, and many can climb trees.

A bear waits to catch salmon
as they leap up a waterfall.

Hunting

Brown bears are one of the biggest bears.
They can hunt huge animals called bison.
Most other bears go after smaller animals
such as birds and rabbits. Some bears
even go fishing in rivers.

Plants and honey

Unlike other big hunters, most bears
don't hunt very often. They prefer food
that is easier to get, such as plants,
insects and honey. But they need to
eat a lot of these to survive.

Pandas spend most of the day
eating bamboo. They eat sitting
down so they don't get tired.

Can you find these bears on the maps?

American black bear
Look in
North America

giant panda
Look in
Asia

sloth bears
Look in
Asia

Asiatic black bear
Look in
Asia

24

Protecting land

Most bears live alone.
Each usually has its
own patch of land
that it guards fiercely
from intruders.

When two bears meet, they may
fight over whose land it is.

Baby bears are born in the winter,
in their mother's den.

Winter dens

In places with freezing winters,
bears normally spend the cold
months asleep in dens. These can
be caves, hollow trees or holes
in the ground or snow.

Treetop bears

Some bears live in forests that are
warm all year round. They are good
climbers and get lots of food from
the trees. Some even sleep
in the treetops.

Spectacled bears use their long
claws to grip onto branches as
they look for food in the forests.

Animals with pouches

Some female animals carry their babies around in pouches. Most of these animals come from Australia.

Kangaroos live in small groups that are mainly made up of mothers and joeys.

Safe pouches

The largest animals with pouches are kangaroos. Baby kangaroos, called joeys, spend half a year growing in their mothers' pouches until they are ready to leave. Even then, young joeys will hop back into the pouch if they are scared.

A female wombat's pouch faces backwards, so she doesn't flick soil at her baby when she digs.

Underground homes

Wombats dig large burrows to live in, with long tunnels and lots of rooms. Most adults have their own burrows, but mothers share theirs with their babies.

Can you find these animals with pouches on the Australasia and Oceania map?

spiny bandicoot

wombat

cuscus

kangaroos

bilby

In the cities

Animals called possums often live in Australian towns and cities. They come out at night and wake people up with their loud clattering and fighting.

Possums use their long toes and sharp claws to scamper along trees and rooftops.

Tasmanian devils try to scare each other away by snarling.

Noisy devils

Tasmanian devils are the biggest hunters with pouches. Their name comes from the scary screeches they make. If they are threatened, they make a strong smell to drive off attackers.

Sleepy koalas

Koalas sleep all day, and most of the night too. But they spend several hours each night climbing through eucalyptus trees, eating leaves.

When a baby koala first leaves its mother's pouch, it's too small to climb so it clings onto her fur.

tree kangaroo

wallaby

Tasmanian devil

possum

Birds

There are many different kinds of birds around the world, but they all have feathers, wings and beaks, and all baby birds hatch from eggs.

A male blue bird of paradise hangs upside down to display his feathers.

Showing off

Male birds often have to try hard to attract a partner. Some sing songs, and others perform complicated dances or show off their amazing feathers.

Hungry chicks open their mouths wide and cheep to beg for food.

Eggs and chicks

Many parent birds work together to raise their chicks. The mother sits on the eggs to keep them warm, and the father takes turns or brings food. When the eggs hatch, both parents find food for the tiny chicks.

Can you find these birds on the maps?

blue jay
Look in
North America

rufous-tailed hummingbird
Look in
South America

rainbow lorikeet
Look in
Australasia and Oceania

golden eagle
Look in
Asia

Feathers

Birds have several kinds of feathers. The soft downy feathers next to their skin keep them warm, while their stiff wing and tail feathers help them to fly and balance.

On cold nights, birds fluff up their downy feathers to trap their body heat.

Wings and flying

Most birds have strong wings and light bodies, which make them good fliers. Some fly long distances each year, to reach places that have better weather or more food.

Birds on long journeys often form a V-shape. They take turns flying at the front.

An emu has tiny wings hidden under its feathers.

Flightless birds

Not all birds can fly. Some used to live in places with no hunters, so didn't need to fly. Others became good runners or swimmers instead. Gradually their wings changed until they couldn't fly at all.

cardinal
Look in
North America

bowerbirds
Look in
Australasia and Oceania

gyrfalcon
Look in
Europe

rhea
Look in
South America

Rivers and lakes

Rivers and lakes are home to lots of different kinds of animals around the world. Visitors gather there too, to eat, drink and cool down.

A kingfisher watches the water closely, waiting for fish to appear.

Water voles' burrows have several entrances, both above and below the water.

On the banks

Many animals live along the edges of rivers and lakes. Kingfishers make holes in the banks each year to lay their eggs in, while water voles, water shrews and otters dig burrows to live in all year round.

Hunter fish

Fish often hunt for food, but most only eat tiny animals, such as insects. However, fiercer fish catch larger prey. Piranhas are fish that hunt in groups and attack animals of all sizes.

Piranhas have sharp teeth for tearing up their prey.

Can you find these animals on the maps?

European kingfisher
Look in
Europe

river dolphin
Look in
South America

hippopotamus
Look in
Africa

great blue heron
Look in
North America

Busy builders

Beavers build dams across rivers to stop the water from flowing. Then they make homes called lodges in the flooded water. They build them out of wood, which they get by cutting down trees with their teeth.

The lodge's entrances are hidden underwater.

This is the dam.

A crocodile's eyes and nostrils are on top of its head. This means it can see and breathe when it's mostly underwater.

Lurking danger

Crocodiles and alligators have greenish-brown skin that helps them to hide in murky water. They look like floating logs as they drift along, waiting for prey.

Mud baths

Elephants, hippopotamuses and rhinoceroses enjoy cooling off in rivers and lakes. When they leave the water, they sometimes coat themselves with mud so their skin doesn't dry out in the sun.

Elephants use their trunks to spray water over themselves.

Seas and oceans

Over half of the world is covered by seas and oceans. Most animals live near the surface where there's lots of light, but some live much further down.

Breathing and leaping

Unlike fish, whales and dolphins can't breathe underwater. They come to the surface and take in air through holes on their heads. Sometimes, whales leap up out of the water again and again, but no one knows why.

It takes a lot of effort for a huge whale to throw itself out of the ocean like this.

Ocean hunters

Sharks need super senses to find their prey in the huge oceans. They have an especially good sense of smell, which helps them to track prey from far away. Some can smell tiny traces of blood, so they can find hurt animals that are easy to catch.

A shark chases its prey by beating its strong tail to move quickly through the water.

Can you find these animals on the maps?

humpback whale
Look in
Europe

moray eel
Look in
Australasia and Oceania

Moorish idol
Look in
Australasia and Oceania

tripod fish
Look in
Africa

Sunny reefs

Coral reefs grow in shallow, sunlit water. They look like bright plants, but really they are made up of tiny animals called corals.

Many creatures live around coral reefs, hiding away in nooks and crannies.

A deep-sea anglerfish has a light on its head, and a big mouth for gulping down its prey.

Dark depths

Much deeper down in the ocean, the water becomes cold and dark. Many animals that live there make their own light. They use it to find each other or to attract prey.

Polar animals

The areas around the North Pole (also known as the Arctic) and the South Pole (or Antarctica) are the coldest in the world. Life can be hard for animals there, especially during the long winters.

Arctic terns spend summer in the Arctic, and then fly to Antarctica for a second summer.

Winter coats

As summer ends in the Arctic, some animals' coats start to turn white. Their new fur will help them to blend in with the winter snow. When the snow thaws, their darker summer coats begin to grow back.

In winter, an Arctic fox's fur turns white and becomes much thicker.

Icefish live near Antarctica. They are very pale and have see-through blood.

Busy waters

A surprising number of animals live in the icy polar oceans. Many fish there have special blood that doesn't freeze in the water. Other animals have thick layers of fat called blubber to keep them warm.

Can you find these polar animals on the Arctic and Antarctica maps?

| snow sheep | narwhal | snow petrel | Adélie penguin | harp seal |

Super swimmers

Penguins spend most of their time in Antarctic oceans. They are birds, but they can't fly. Instead they use their wings as flippers for swimming. Every year, they come onto land to lay their eggs.

On land, penguins walk clumsily or slide on their tummies.

Breathing holes

In winter, huge sheets of ice form over the oceans. Seals swim in the water, but they have to stay near holes in the ice so they can come up to breathe.

When a seal leaves the water, it stays near an ice hole so it can dive in to escape from hunters.

A polar bear paddles with its strong front legs. Its back legs help it to steer.

Arctic hunting

Polar bears hunt on the ice sheets. They creep up on prey or wait by breathing holes. When the sheets start to melt, they swim between floating patches of ice.

Night animals

Some animals sleep during the day and come out at night, when it's easier to creep around without being seen. Night animals need super senses to get around safely and find food in the dark.

Listening for echoes

Bats use sound to discover what's around them. They make high squeaks, and listen for the echoes. The amount of time it takes for an echo to bounce back tells them how far away things are.

Bats have big ears that can pick up very quiet echoes.

Night light

Many night animals have big eyes, to help them see in the dark. Some animals also have layers at the back of their eyes that reflect light. This helps them to make the most of even very small amounts of light.

A bushbaby's eyes reflect light, making them look as if they are glowing.

Can you find these night animals on the maps?

barn owl
Look in
Europe

hedgehog
Look in
Europe

tarsier
Look in
Asia

free-tailed bat
Look in
North America

red fox
Look in
Europe

A chinchilla's whiskers are especially long and thick, helping it to feel its surroundings.

Sensitive whiskers

Many animals have long, stiff hairs called whiskers on their faces. Animals can sense when these touch something, even very lightly. This helps them to feel their way through the dark.

An owl flies so quietly that its prey doesn't hear it coming.

Diving for prey

Owls have excellent hearing and sight for night hunting. When they spot their prey, they swoop down and grab it with their claws. Soft feathers on their legs muffle any noise they make as they dive.

Creepy crawlies

There are billions and billions of creepy crawlies all over the world. Many hide away under the ground or beneath logs and rocks, but others are easier to spot.

Termites are tiny, but big groups of them build giant mounds to live in.

Counting legs

The most common creepy crawlies are insects, which have six legs and can usually fly. Spiders have eight legs, and millipedes can have hundreds, arranged in pairs down their bodies.

Although a millipede has many legs, they are very short so it can only move slowly.

Working together

Leafcutter ants collect pieces of leaves to grow food on in their underground nest.

Some insects live in huge groups where each one does a job, such as finding food, standing guard or feeding babies. A big female called the queen lays all the group's eggs.

Can you find these creepy crawlies on the maps?

garden spider
Look in
Europe

weta
Look in
Australasia and Oceania

scarab beetle
Look in
Africa

blue morpho butterfly
Look in
South America

Spinning webs

Spiders are hunters, and many build webs to catch their prey. They carefully spin the webs from threads they make inside their bodies. When a web is finished, the spider waits for insects to fly into it.

When a fly gets caught, the spider feels the web shaking.

Flowers and seeds

Bees suck up nectar and take it to their nests to make honey.

Flowers make a juice called nectar, which some insects drink. Flowers also make pollen dust. As insects fly around collecting nectar, they help to spread the pollen. When pollen lands on other flowers, they use it to make seeds.

Changing shape

Many insects change completely as they grow up. Baby insects don't have wings, and some don't have legs. When a baby is ready to become an adult, it makes a case around itself and changes shape inside it.

A caterpillar starts off small, but grows quickly.

It makes a case, and slowly turns into a butterfly inside it.

The butterfly climbs out and dries its wings before flying away.

Caterpillar

Butterfly

Case

Poisonous animals

There are poisonous animals in most parts of the world. They use their poison to protect themselves from hunters or to catch prey. Poison that is injected using fangs or stingers is called venom.

Snakebites

When a poisonous snake bites its prey, venom drips down its fangs into the wound. This causes pain and swelling or stops the prey from moving. The strongest venom can kill.

A viper's fangs usually lie flat in the top of its mouth. But when it gets ready to bite, they flip down like this.

If a scorpion is threatened, it prepares to strike by raising its stinger.

Stinger

Sting in the tail

Scorpions have curly tails with poisonous stingers at the end, which they flick forward to sting attackers or prey. But making venom takes lots of energy, so they use as little as possible.

Can you find these poisonous animals on the maps?

Russell's viper
Look in
Asia

Brazilian wandering spider
Look in
South America

stonefish
Look in
Asia

Arizona desert scorpion
Look in
North America

Stinging tentacles

Box jellyfish have long tentacles with stingers on them. They spread out their tentacles and wait for prey to brush against them. Their venom stops the prey from moving, so the jellyfish can swallow it easily.

Box jellyfish have see-through bodies, so it's hard for prey to spot them.

A puffer fish swallows lots of water very quickly to make itself swell up.

Puffed-up fish

Some puffer fish are very poisonous when eaten. To avoid being eaten at all, they swell up to three times their usual size. Then they are too big for a hunter to fit in its mouth.

Warning marks

Many poisonous animals have bright patterns. If another animal is stung by them or eats them and becomes sick, it remembers the pattern. Next time it sees a pattern like that, it will stay away.

Even in thick rainforests, the bright skin of a poison dart frog is easy to spot.

black widow spider

Look in
North America

cane toad

Look in
South America

redback spider

Look in
Australasia and Oceania

Egyptian cobra

Look in
Africa

Baby animals

Baby animals usually grow inside their mothers' bodies, or inside eggs that their mothers lay. Although many babies stay with their parents for a long time, others have to take care of themselves from the start.

Eggs and shells

Eggs that are laid on land have shells, to stop their insides from drying out. But eggs laid in water are usually smaller and softer, with no shell around them.

Sea turtles leave the water to lay their eggs. They bury them in the sand and then leave, so they never see their babies.

A male sea horse carries hundreds of eggs in a pouch. When the babies hatch, they leave in big groups.

Lone fathers

With some kinds of animals, the males take care of the eggs on their own. They make nests to keep the eggs in, or carry them around. When the eggs hatch, some fathers take care of the babies too.

Helpless babies

At first, many baby animals
can't walk, see or hear.
Some can't eat solid food,
so they drink milk from
their mothers instead.

Wolf cubs can't see
or hear for over a week
after being born, so they
stay close to their mother.

Playtime

Young animals learn by playing games.
Baby hunters play at fighting, sneaking around
and chasing, while animals that are hunted spend
more time running and kicking. In big groups,
playing together helps babies to get to know
each other better too.

Baby meerkats play
together, while an adult
watches out for danger.

Animal quiz

How much have you discovered about animals around the world? Try this quiz to find out. The answers are on page 48.

Animal homes

Where do these animals often live?

1. cheetahs
2. possums
3. spectacled bears

a. towns and cities
b. forests
c. grasslands

Which animal?

1. Which birds spend time in both the Arctic and Antarctica?

2. Which animals have fangs that flip down when they get ready to bite?

3. What are the largest animals with pouches?

4. Which big cats live in groups?

Feeding time

Can you match these animals
with the food they eat?

1. pandas
2. bees
3. monkeys
4. koalas

a. nectar
b. bamboo
c. fruit
d. eucalyptus
   leaves

Baby names

What are the babies of
these animals called?

1. wolves
2. butterflies
3. birds
4. kangaroos

a. chicks
b. caterpillars
c. joeys
d. cubs

Map hunt

Use these clues to help
you find the animals
on the maps.

1. A monster that lives
in North America.

2. A dragon that lives
in Asia.

3. Two kinds of devils
that live in Australasia.

Index of animals

General index

Answers

Animal homes
1. c. grasslands
2. a. towns and cities
3. b. forests

Which animal?
1. Arctic terns
2. vipers
3. kangaroos
4. lions

Feeding time
1. b. bamboo
2. a. nectar
3. c. fruit
4. d. eucalyptus leaves

Baby names
1. d. cubs
2. b. caterpillars
3. a. chicks
4. c. joeys

Map hunt
1. gila monster
2. Komodo dragon
3. Tasmanian devil and thorny devil

Image manipulation by Nick Wakeford and Will Dawes

First published in 2008 by Usborne Publishing Ltd, 83–85 Saffron Hill, London EC1N 8RT, England.
www.usborne.com Copyright © 2008 Usborne Publishing Ltd.
The name Usborne and the devices ♀ ⊕ are Trade Marks of Usborne Publishing Ltd. All rights reserved.
No part of this publication may be reproduced, stored in a retrieval system, or transmitted in any form or by any means,
electronic, mechanical, photocopying, recording or otherwise, without the prior permission of the publisher. UE.
First published in America 2008. Printed in UAE.